Man and Mustang

Photographs and text by George Ancona

Macmillan Publishing Company
New York

Maxwell Macmillan Canada
Toronto

Maxwell Macmillan International
New York   Oxford   Singapore   Sydney

To Helga

Macmillan Publishing Company is part of the Maxwell Communication Group of Companies.

Macmillan Publishing Company, 866 Third Avenue, New York, NY 10022.

Maxwell Macmillan Canada, Inc., 1200 Eglinton Avenue East, Suite 200, Don Mills, Ontario M3C 3N1.

First edition
Printed in the United States of America

10   9   8   7   6   5   4   3   2   1

The text of this book is set in 14 pt. ITC Cushing Book.

Library of Congress Cataloging-in-Publication Data
Ancona, George.
Man and mustang / photographs and text by George Ancona. — 1st ed.
       p.   cm.
Summary: Describes the government program which maintains an ecological balance among wild mustangs by capturing, training, and offering for adoption selected animals.
ISBN 0-02-700802-9
1. United States. Bureau of Land Management. Adopt-A-Horse or Burro—Juvenile literature.   2. Wild horse adoption—West (U.S.)—Juvenile literature.   3. Mustang—Juvenile literature.   [1. United States. Bureau of Land Management. Adopt-A-Horse or Burro.   2. Wild horse adoption.   3. Mustang.   4. Wildlife conservation.]   I. Title.
SF360.4.A53   1992   636.1′3—dc20   91-29513

Five hundred years ago, the Spanish conquistadores landed on the Western Hemisphere with their horses. Although the horse's ancestor, Eohippus, roamed North America about 50 million years ago, for some unknown reason horses had disappeared from here. With horses, burros, and oxen, the Spanish were able to journey far afield, exploring, conquering, and settling this land. They were a formidable foe for the native Americans they encountered.

During the two hundred years it took the Spanish to inhabit the Southwest, many of their horses escaped into the wilderness. Today the animals' descendants are running free on remote public lands of the western states. These wild horses are called mustangs.

The Bureau of Land Management (BLM), a government agency, was formed to control the grazing of livestock on public lands. Today the BLM's job is to maintain an ecological balance among wild horse and other wildlife habitats; cattle and sheep grazing; timber, coal, gas, and oil

production; and public recreation such as hunting, fishing, camping, and rock climbing.

Once, wild horses and burros were not considered native wildlife and therefore were not protected. They were hunted and slaughtered for dog food. But in 1971 Congress passed the Wild Free-Roaming Horse and Burro Act to protect these animals. And now, since the horse's natural predators, such as the wolf, have been almost eradicated, mustangs are flourishing.

Every winter, wild horse specialists from the BLM fly over large tracts of western range lands to count the population of mustangs and burros. The animals are easily seen against the snow. Then the BLM evaluates the quality of the habitat and determines how much forage it can produce. If the horse population is too big for the land to support, the BLM will reduce the herds. The horses and burros that are removed are offered to the public through the bureau's Adopt-A-Horse program.

The BLM office in Ely, Nevada, manages the lands of the Great Basin that lie in the east central part of the state. After four years of drought and overgrazing, the nutritious white sage and perennial grasses there have been reduced to short, stubby plants—not enough forage to feed all the grazing animals. To preserve both the land and the mustangs, the BLM decides to remove 390 horses.

The gathering, or roundup of horses, takes place any time after June. Most foals are born in the spring and by July are strong enough to run with the herd and big enough to be kept in close quarters without being hurt.

The BLM hires Dave Cattoor, a roundup expert, to carry out the gathering. Dave has his wranglers set up a corral hidden behind a hill. The wranglers, cowboys who work mostly with horses, use coarse burlap to camouflage the two wings of fencing at the entrance to the trap. The corral probably will be moved to other locations so that the BLM can capture its quota of mustangs.

The BLM uses helicopters to find the mustangs and herd them into the traps. Cliff Heaverne, the pilot-wrangler, takes off at the first light of day. A second chopper follows, carrying Bob Brown, one of the two BLM specialists who attend the gathering. He is there to see that the animals are not run too hard or abused in any other way.

During droughts, the horses migrate long distances looking for pasture and water. Cliff begins his search by flying over the wooded hills that surround the valley. Once he spots a band of horses, it may take hours for him to coax them from the safety of the trees and down to the trap. Cliff knows horses; he has worked with them all his life.

At the trap, Sheree Kahle—the second BLM wild horse specialist—stays in touch with the two helicopters by radio. Each day she and her partner, Bob, take turns flying in the observation helicopter.

The first warning of action is the faint hum of the distant helicopter. Looking out over the valley, the wranglers at the trap see the dust that signals the approach of horses. Then they spot Cliff, who stays well behind the horses to keep them moving at an easy lope.

The radio in the BLM pickup crackles with Cliff's voice, warning the ground crew of his arrival. The wranglers move into their positions behind the burlap-covered fences. Dave Cattoor calls to his grandson to bring his mare, Cricket, out to the middle of the two wings of fencing. Cricket will act as a pilot horse, guiding the frightened mustangs into the trap.

All is still and ready as the sound of the helicopter grows louder.

Suddenly, over the crest of the hill the leaders of the mustang band appear, galloping as Cliff brings his roaring chopper closer to them. Dave slaps Cricket on the rump and hides behind a sagebrush. The mare trots easily into the corral. The lead mustangs see and follow her into the trap.

As the last mustang enters the corral, the waiting wranglers spring out from their hiding places. To keep the horses in the corral, the men shout and wave long wands with white rags on the ends until they can close the gates on the bewildered horses.

Their days of freedom over, the skittish horses circle and paw the dust of the corral. They search in vain for an escape route from their trap and the strange two-legged creatures around them.

A band of mustangs consists of the male leader—a stallion—and several mares and their foals. Young stallions will stay with the band until they are old enough to challenge the leader or move out to form bands of their own.

Each time a band is captured, the wranglers climb up onto the corral fence to count the mustangs while Bob records the tally. Then the wranglers separate the horses into three groups for shipping. The stallions go into one pen, the mares into another, and the foals and yearlings into a third. This keeps the stallions from fighting over the mares, and the young ones from being injured by the larger horses. In the pens, they are fed hay and water.

As soon as enough horses have been captured, a livestock tractor trailer is backed up to the corral's loading chute. Bob and Sheree check the condition of the animals to make sure they are healthy enough to be shipped. Sick animals are destroyed. The truck holds forty horses, which remain separated in the three groups. Once the truck has been loaded, its doors close, and the mustangs begin the journey away from their native lands.

After a six-hour drive, the horses arrive at the Palomino Valley Wild Horse and Burro Placement Center near Reno, Nevada. There each horse is isolated in a padded chute so it can be examined by the veterinarian. He determines the horse's age by looking at its teeth. Then he draws blood to test for parasites, vaccinates it against equine diseases, and gives it medicine for worms.

The vet will also castrate young stallions to make them less aggressive and easier to train. Male horses that have had their testicles removed are called geldings.

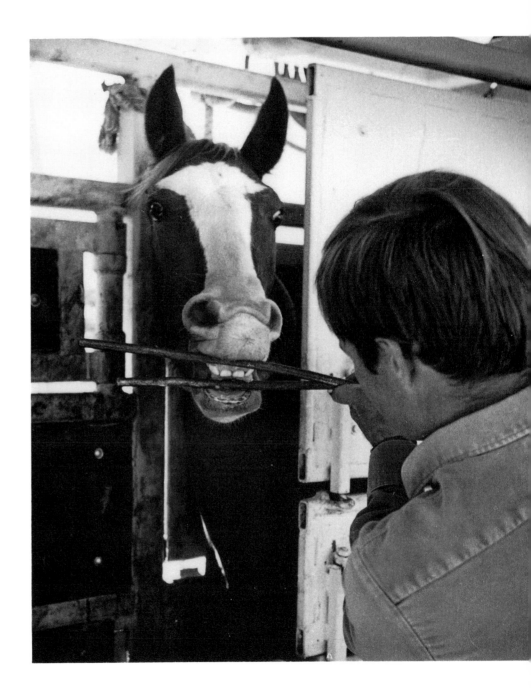

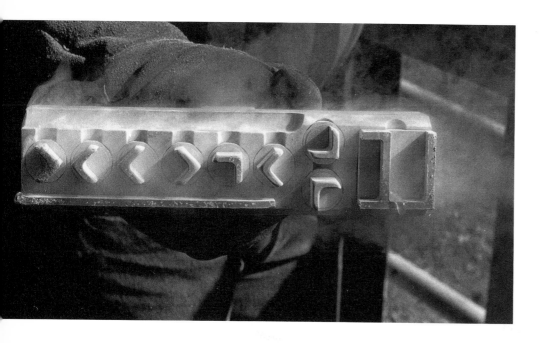

Each horse is given a number, which is freeze-branded on its neck by a wrangler. Instead of numerals, the brand uses alpha-angle symbols to show the horse's year of birth, capture state, and ID number. Liquid nitrogen lowers the temperature of the brand to minus 300 degrees Fahrenheit. The freeze mark is less painful than red-hot irons for branding animals. The information about the horse is also entered into a computer, and the ID number is put on a plastic tag tied to the horse's neck.

A few horses stay in Palomino Valley; the rest are sent to other adoption centers around the country. Some of the centers are at western prisons. The BLM has made arrangements with these prisons to allow inmates to train and gentle the mustangs for adoption.

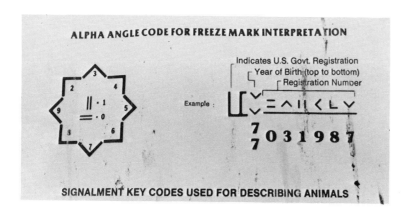

ALPHA ANGLE CODE FOR FREEZE MARK INTERPRETATION

Indicates U.S. Govt. Registration
Year of Birth (top to bottom)
Registration Number

Example:

7 031987

SIGNALMENT KEY CODES USED FOR DESCRIBING ANIMALS

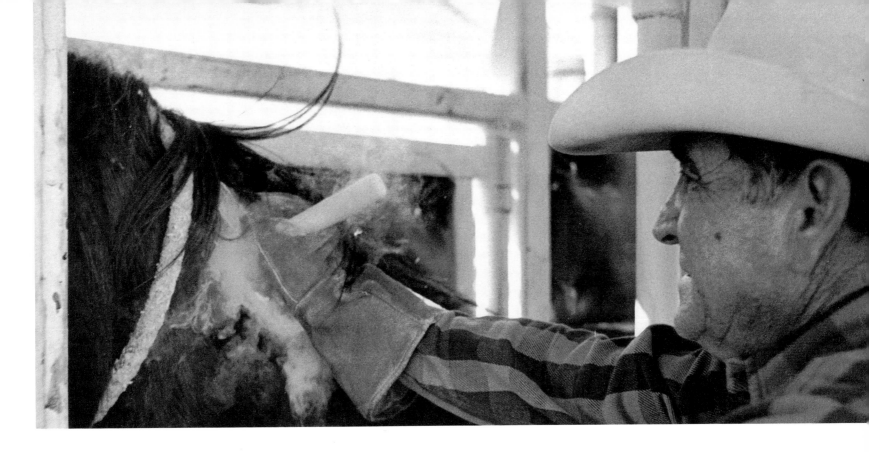

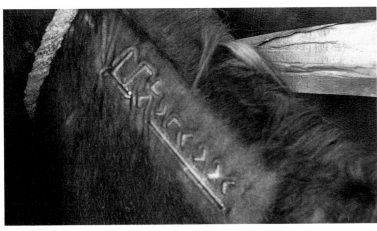

Just outside of Santa Fe stand the high walls and guard towers of the New Mexico State Penitentiary. They overlook the corrals of the BLM Adopt-A-Horse program.

The horses shipped from Nevada arrive at the prison after a twenty-four-hour trip. They are coaxed out of the trailer and down the chute to the corrals that will be their home for the next few months. The mustangs huddle together, uncertain until they see the feeding troughs. Then they settle down to eat and drink.

For the first few weeks, the mustangs are allowed to get used to their new home. In the beginning they run away from the men who bring them their food. But after a while they realize that humans are the source of their meals.

Every morning Jess Hollar, the assistant wrangler, and his dog, Orphan, pick up a group of prisoners in an old school bus and take them to the corrals. Both Jess and his boss, Rod Jeffers, teach the men how to work with horses. The minimum-security prisoners are volunteers who prefer working with wild horses to spending their days inside the prison walls.

When they first meet, the men and the mustangs are wary of each other. Jess has seen men come into the corrals tough, arrogant, and "with an attitude." They usually change, because to gain the animals' trust, the men must be patient and gentle.

Each inmate trainer is assigned a horse to work with. A "green" inmate will work alongside a more experienced trainer under the wranglers' watchful eyes. As Jess says, "No hundred-and-fifty-pound man can make an eleven-hundred-pound horse do anything it doesn't want to." Only by working with the horse eight hours a day, feeding, talking, caring, can the man win over the animal.

Training begins when a horse is moved into a narrow chute and a gate is closed behind it. This restricts the mustang's movement so that a trainer can get close safely. Erv Benally, one of the more experienced trainers, climbs up onto a platform alongside the chute. In his hand he has a halter with a thick, twenty-foot rope attached. With gentle words, Erv eases the halter under the frightened horse's nose, then brings the strap over the head and buckles it closed. He moves cautiously because a wild horse is unpredictable.

A less experienced trainer sometimes provokes a horse's fear. The horse might then rear up or try to bite the man in its attempt to escape the chute.

The most dangerous time for any trainer is when the horse is released from the chute. Then trainers often work in teams. While one man holds on to the end of the halter rope, another opens the chute. The horse leaps out and pulls, bucks, rears, trying desperately to get away, but the trainer holds on, keeping the rope taut. If he needs help, the other trainer will grab the rope. The halter and the rope are the means by which the man gets the horse to do his bidding. After a while, the horse tires and stops its futile struggle. Holding still, man and mustang stand eyeing each other.

While maintaining eye contact and talking, the trainer moves hand over hand across the rope, ready for any sudden pull. With luck, the trainer reaches the horse and touches its nose. He then leads the horse out of the chute area and into an enclosed round pen for the next lesson.

The enclosed pen screens out distractions. And because it is round, there is no corner for the horse to hide in. Here the horse will learn to respond to the halter rope.

First Erv runs the mare in one direction, then in the opposite. Holding the rope closer to the horse, he uses the free end to brush against her side, or snaps it to encourage her to run.

After running, Erv walks the horse around the pen, pulling her head from side to side, getting her used to being led by the halter rope. Later Erv drapes a burlap sack over the rope and then over the horse to accustom her to new experiences. He ends the lesson by standing in front of the horse, where, with soothing words and easy gestures, he reaches out and pets her.

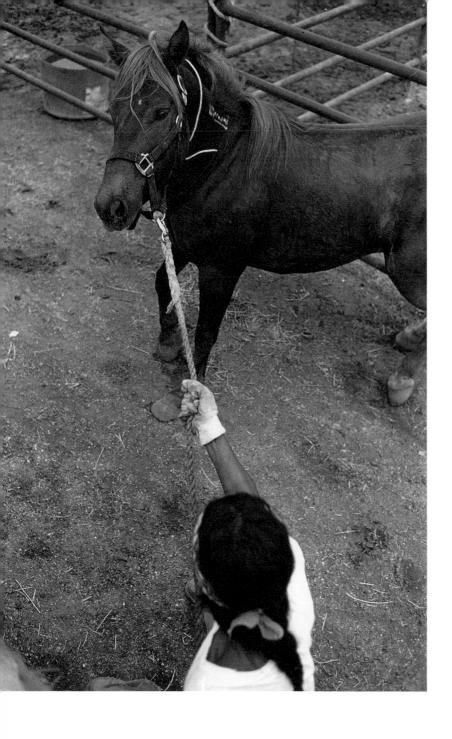

After the training session in the enclosed corral, Erv takes the mare to her own pen to rest. He passes the halter rope through a rubber inner tube tied to a corner post. When the horse pulls against the rope, the tube stretches and prevents her from hurting herself.

To prepare the horse for a human's care, Erv puts his glove on a stick and begins to stroke her. Saying, "Easy, now. It's all right," he moves the glove along the horse's body. On other days he uses a curry comb instead of the glove. In time the horse will actually enjoy being groomed.

The next training phase takes place in an open round pen, where a horse can see everything that goes on. Here the trainer teaches the horse to follow directions regardless of distractions.

By closing a pen's gate against a tethered horse, a trainer can safely pet and comb it. Once the horse understands that the man won't hurt it and begins to trust him, it will accept the man's care. Erv often sits and just talks to his mare. Eventually his voice reassures the mustang and prepares her for voice commands like *walk*, *trot*, *canter*, and *whoa*.

Some mustangs can be gentled in as little as a week, while others take up to a month. Older horses that cannot be gentled are sent to a sanctuary, where they live out their lives in a protected habitat.

For some of the inmate trainers, the big event of the year is the New Mexico State Fair. It is their chance to join the world outside the prison walls and to show the results of their work. Their horses have been gentled and are ready for adoption. The trainers express their affection.

To prepare for the fair, the men shampoo the mustangs and trim the hair from their manes, tails, fetlocks, whiskers, and ears. Then they comb and brush the horses until their coats glisten in the sun. Finally they give their horses one last workout before parading into the ring.

One day of the fair is devoted to the showing of mustangs. People come from near and far to exhibit their adopted horses and what they've taught them. These horses have been broken to the saddle and bit and are used for pleasure riding and for working on ranches.

The horses and trainers from the New Mexico state prisons enter the Inmate Halter Class competition. In this event, the trainers line up with their horses in front of the judge. Each man is asked to lead his horse by the halter in a walk and a trot, and then to stop the horse in a squared-up position, that is, with four feet planted on the ground and its head held high. This shows the horse to its best advantage.

The trainers whose horses perform best win trophies and ribbons, and they leave the ring grinning with pride.

People who are interested in adopting a mustang visit the prison corrals to look over the horses. Dave Whitlock and his family have already adopted two horses and want two more so that each member of the family will have a horse to ride. Rod Jeffers takes them around, describing the personalities of the different horses. Like people, horses vary in personality, temperament, and intelligence. Rod and Jess know the horses and can recommend the right ones for the family.

The Whitlocks choose the mare that Erv is training. She can now be led by the halter. They watch as Erv ties a rope to a hoof to raise it. He repeats this with each hoof. Soon he will be able to do it by hand so that the hooves can be trimmed and shod. Then the horse will be ready for adoption.

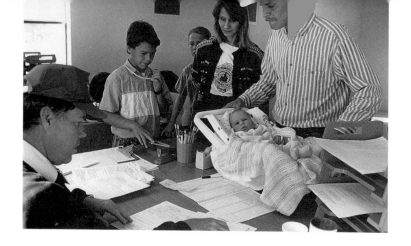

The day arrives when Erv's horse is gentled and the Whitlocks come to pick her up. The mare is accompanied by her colt at no extra charge. The entire family appears to pay the $125 to John Arwood, the BLM representative, and to sign the adoption papers. According to the papers, if the horses are not properly cared for, the BLM will take them back.

When the horses have been loaded into the trailer, Erv offers some last-minute advice to the Whitlocks. Before closing the door, he gives his mare a rub on the nose and says, "Bye, Momma. Take care of your baby." Erv will stay to finish serving his sentence. He hopes to use his horse-training skills after his release.

Far from their birthplace and gentled, the
mustangs leave the second world they have known.
They will continue to live among people, but now
they are part of a family.

For further information on how you can adopt a mustang or burro, contact one of the nearest Bureau of Land Management Wild Horse and Burro Adoption Centers.

ARIZONA
Kingman Corrals
Phoenix, Arizona
(602) 757-3161

CALIFORNIA
Ridgecrest Corrals
Ridgecrest, California
(619) 446-6064

California State Office
Sacramento, California
(916) 978-4725

Litchfield Corrals
Susanville, California
(914) 254-6762

MONTANA
Britton Springs Corrals
Mile City, Montana
(307) 548-2706

NEVADA
Palomino Valley Corrals
Palomino Valley, Nevada
(702) 673-1150

NEW MEXICO
Albuquerque District Office
Albuquerque, New Mexico
(505) 761-8700

New Mexico State Office
Santa Fe, New Mexico
(505) 988-6231

OREGON
Burns Corrals
Burns, Oregon
(503) 573-5241

PENNSYLVANIA
Northeastern Adoption Center
Lewisberry, Pennsylvania
(717) 938-8030

TENNESSEE
Southeastern Adoption Center
Cross Plains, Tennessee
(615) 654-2180

VIRGINIA
Eastern States Office
Alexandria, Virginia
(703) 274-0232

WYOMING
Rock Springs Corrals
Rock Springs, Wyoming
(307) 382-5350

THANKS to the many people who helped me with this book: To John Arwood of the Albuquerque BLM Office, who introduced me to Rod Jeffers and Jess Hollar, the program's horse trainers at the Santa Fe Penitentiary, and who read the manuscript for me. To Warden Robert Tamsy and Don Caviness of the New Mexico Department of Corrections, who facilitated my photography at the prison. To the people of the Nevada BLM, Fred Wolf, Tom Pogacnic, and Ken Walker. In Ely, to Bob Brown, who reviewed the manuscript, Sheree Kahle, and Jerry Smith, who all guided me during the gatherings. To Dave Cattoor and Cliff Heaverne of Helicopter Roundups. In Palomino Valley, to Fred Wyatt, who showed me around and introduced me to Dr. Richard Sanford, the vet, and the wranglers, Buck Mangus and Lindon Albright, and to Maxine Shane, who paved the way for my visit. To Helga Ancona, who helped with the early research and photography. To Lynn Zinser, who taught me about horses. To the Caballeros de Vargas for the conquistadores. To the Whitlock family, who graciously invited me to their home. And last but not least, to the men of the Santa Fe Penitentiary, who allowed me to photograph them as they risked their necks working with wild horses. I'm grateful to you all.

George Ancona